GDB
Pocket Reference

GDB
Pocket Reference

Arnold Robbins

Beijing · Cambridge · Farnham · Köln · Sebastopol · Tokyo

GDB Pocket Reference
by Arnold Robbins

Copyright © 2005 O'Reilly Media, Inc. All rights reserved.
Printed in the United States of America.

Published by O'Reilly Media, Inc., 1005 Gravenstein Highway North,
Sebastopol, CA 95472.

O'Reilly books may be purchased for educational, business, or sales
promotional use. Online editions are also available for most titles
(*safari.oreilly.com*). For more information, contact our corporate/
institutional sales department: (800) 998-9938 or *corporate@oreilly.com*.

Editor:	Mike Loukides
Production Editor:	Claire Cloutier
Cover Designer:	Emma Colby
Interior Designer:	David Futato

Printing History:

May 2005:	First Edition.

ISBN: 978-0-596-10027-8
[LSI]   [2011-04-29]

GDB
Pocket Reference

Arnold Robbins

Beijing · Cambridge · Farnham · Köln · Sebastopol · Tokyo

GDB Pocket Reference
by Arnold Robbins

Copyright © 2005 O'Reilly Media, Inc. All rights reserved.
Printed in the United States of America.

Published by O'Reilly Media, Inc., 1005 Gravenstein Highway North,
Sebastopol, CA 95472.

Editor:	Mike Loukides
Production Editor:	Claire Cloutier
Cover Designer:	Emma Colby
Interior Designer:	David Futato

Printing History:

May 2005:   First Edition.

ISBN: 978-0-596-10027-8
[LSI]   [2011-04-29]

Table of Contents

GDB Pocket Reference

Introduction

The GNU Debugger, GDB, is the standard debugger on GNU/Linux and BSD systems and can be used on just about any Unix system with a C compiler and at least one of several well-known object file formats. It can also be used on other kinds of systems as well. GDB has a very rich feature set, making it the preferred debugger of many developers the world over.

This pocket reference provides a complete summary of GDB command-line syntax, initialization files, expressions, variables, and commands. It also describes the source code locations for GDB and two other graphical debuggers based on GDB.

A full introduction to GDB may be found in its documentation, which is included in the source code. This documentation is also available from the Free Software Foundation in *Debugging with GDB: The GNU Source-Level Debugger*, by Richard M. Stallman, Roland Pesch, Stan Shebs, et al.

Conventions Used in This Book

This book follows the typographic conventions that are outlined below:

Constant width

> Used for directory names, commands, program names, functions, variables, and options. All terms shown in constant width are typed literally. It is also used to show the contents of files or the output from commands.

Constant width italic

> Used in syntax and command summaries to show generic text; these should be replaced with user-supplied values.

Constant width bold

> Used in examples to show text that should be typed literally by the user.

Italic

> Used to show generic arguments and options; these should be replaced with user-supplied values. Italic is also used to indicate URLs, macro package names, filenames, comments in examples, and the first mention of terms.

$

> Used in some examples as the Bash, Bourne or Korn shell prompt.

program(N)

> Indicates the "manpage" for *program* in section *N* of the online manual. For example, *echo*(1) means the entry for the echo command.

[ ]

> Surround optional elements in a description of syntax. (The brackets themselves should never be typed.) Note that many commands show the argument [*files*]. If a filename is omitted, standard input (usually the keyboard) is assumed. End keyboard input with an end-of-file character.

---

^x

indicates a "control character," typed by holding down the Control key and the *x* key for any key *x*.

|

Used in syntax descriptions to separate items for which only one alternative may be chosen at a time.

Conceptual Overview

A *debugger* is a program that lets you run a second program, which we will call the *debuggee*. The debugger lets you examine and change the state of the debuggee, and control its execution. In particular, you can *single-step* the program, executing one statement or instruction at a time, in order to watch the program's behavior.

Debuggers come in two flavors: *instruction-level debuggers*, which work at the level of machine instructions, and *source-level debuggers*, which operate in terms of your program's source code and programming language. The latter are considerably easier to use, and usually can do machine-level debugging if necessary. GDB is a source-level debugger; it is probably the most widely applicable (portable to the largest number of architectures) of any current debugger.

GDB itself provides two user interfaces: the traditional command-line interface (CLI) and a text user interface (TUI). The latter is meant for regular terminals or terminal emulators, dividing the screen into separate "windows" for the display of source code, register values, and so on.

GDB provides support for debugging programs written in C, C++, Objective C, Java™,* and Fortran. It provides partial support for Modula-2 programs compiled with the GNU

---

* GDB can only debug Java programs that have been compiled to native machine code with GJC, the GNU Java compiler (part of GCC, the GNU Compiler Collection).

Modula-2 compiler and for Ada programs compiled with the GNU Ada Translator, GNAT. GDB provides some minimal support for debugging Pascal programs. The Chill language is no longer supported.

When working with C++ and Objective C, GDB provides *name demangling*. C++ and Objective C encode overloaded procedure names into a unique "mangled" name that represents the procedure's return type, argument types, and class membership. This ensures so-called *type-safe linkage*. There are different methods for name mangling, thus GDB allows you to select among a set of supported methods, besides just automatically demangling names in displays.

If your program is compiled with the GNU Compiler Collection (GCC), using the `-g3` and `-gdwarf-2` options, GDB understands references to C preprocessor macros. This is particularly helpful for code using macros to simplify complicated `struct` and `union` members. GDB itself also has partial support for expanding preprocessor macros, with more support planned.

GDB allows you to specify several different kinds of files when doing debugging:

- The *exec file* is the executable program to be debugged— i.e., your program.

- The optional *core file* is a memory dump generated by the program when it dies; this is used, together with the exec file, for postmortem debugging. Core files are usually named `core` on commercial Unix systems. On BSD systems, they are named *program*`.core`. On GNU/Linux systems, they are named `core.`*PID*, where *PID* represents the process ID number. This lets you keep multiple core dumps, if necessary.

- The *symbol file* is a separate file from which GDB can read symbol information: information describing variable names, types, sizes, and locations in the executable

file. GDB, not the compiler, creates these files if necessary. Symbol files are rather esoteric; they're not necessary for run-of-the-mill debugging.

There are different ways to stop your program:

- A *breakpoint* specifies that execution should stop at a particular source code location.
- A *watchpoint* indicates that execution should stop when a particular memory location changes value. The location can be specified either as a regular variable name or via an expression (such as one involving pointers). If hardware assistance for watchpoints is available, GDB uses it, making the cost of using watchpoints small. If it is not available, GDB uses virtual memory techniques, if possible, to implement watchpoints. This also keeps the cost down. Otherwise, GDB implements watchpoints in software by single-stepping the program (executing one instruction at a time).
- A *catchpoint* specifies that execution should stop when a particular event occurs.

The GDB documentation and command set often use the word *breakpoint* as a generic term to mean all three kinds of program stoppers. In particular, use the same commands to enable, disable, and remove all three.

GDB applies different statuses to breakpoints (and watchpoints and catchpoints). They may be *enabled*, which means that the program stops when the breakpoint is hit (or *fires*); *disabled*, which means that GDB keeps track of them but that they don't affect execution; or *deleted*, which means that GDB forgets about them completely. As a special case, breakpoints can be enabled only once. Such a breakpoint stops execution when it is encountered, then becomes disabled (but not forgotten).

Breakpoints may have conditions associated with them. When execution reaches the breakpoint, GDB checks the condition, stopping the program only if the condition is true.

Breakpoints may also have an *ignore count*, which is a count of how many times GDB should ignore the breakpoint when it's reached. As long as a breakpoint's ignore count is non-zero, GDB does not bother checking any condition associated with the breakpoint.

Perhaps the most fundamental concept for working with GDB is that of the *frame*. This is short for *stack frame*, a term from the compiler field. A stack frame is the collection of information needed for each separate function invocation. It contains the function's parameters and local variables, as well as *linkage* information indicating where return values should be placed and the location to which the function should return. GDB assigns numbers to frames, starting at 0 and going up. Frame 0 is the innermost frame—i.e., the function most recently called.

GDB uses the *readline* library, as does the Bash shell, to provide command history, command completion, and interactive editing of the command line. Both Emacs- and vi-style editing commands are available.

Finally, GDB has many features of a programming language. You can define your own variables and apply common programming language operators to them. You can also define your own commands. Additionally, you can define special *hook* commands, which are user-defined commands that GDB executes before or after running a built-in command. (See the entry for **define** in the later section "Alphabetical Summary of GDB Commands" for more details on this.) You can also create while loops and test conditions with if ... else ... end.

GDB is typically used to debug programs on the same machine (*host*) on which it's running. GDB can also be configured for *cross-debugging*—i.e., controlling a remote debuggee with a possibly different machine architecture (the *target*). Remote targets are usually connected to the host via

a serial port or a network connection. Such use is rather esoteric and is therefore not covered here. See the GDB documentation for the full details.

Source Code Locations

GDB is the default debugger on GNU/Linux and BSD systems. It is usable on just about any modern Unix system,
though, as well as many older ones. (However, if your system is really ancient, you may need to fall back to an older
version of GDB.) Besides the command-line and text user
interfaces built in to GDB, there are other programs that provide GUI debuggers. Two of the more popular ones are ddd
(the Data Display Debugger) and Insight. Both of these use
GDB to provide the underlying debugging functionality.
Source code URLs for these programs are listed in the following table.

Debugger	Location
ddd	*ftp://ftp.gnu.org/gnu/ddd/*
GDB	*ftp://ftp.gnu.org/gnu/gdb/*
Insight	*http://sources.redhat.com/insight/*

Command-Line Syntax

GDB is invoked as follows:

```
gdb [options] [executable [corefile-or-PID]]
gdb [options] --args executable [program args ...]
```

The gdbtui command is equivalent to gdb --tui; it invokes
GDB with the Text User Interface (TUI). The TUI is
described in the later section "The GDB Text User Interface."

GDB has both traditional short options and GNU-style long
options. Long options may start with either one or two
hyphens. The command-line options are as follows.

`--args`

> Pass on arguments after *executable* to the program being debugged.

`--async`, `--noasync`

> Enable/disable the asynchronous version of the command-line interface.

`-b` *baudrate*, `--baud` *baudrate*

> Set the serial port baud rate used for remote debugging.

`--batch`

> Process options and then exit.

`--cd` *dir*

> Change current directory to *dir*.

`-c` *file*, `--core` *file*

> Analyze the core dump *file*.

`-d` *dir*, `--directory` *dir*

> Search for source files in *dir*.

`-e` *file*, `--exec` *file*

> Use *file* as the executable.

`-f`, `--fullname`

> Output information used by the Emacs-GDB interface.

`--help`

> Print a usage and option summary and then exit.

`--interpreter` *interp*

> Select a specific interpreter/user interface. The command-line interface is the default, although there are other interfaces for use by frontend programs.

`-m`, `--mapped`

> Use mapped symbol files if supported on this system.

`-n`, `--nx`

> Do not read the *.gdbinit* file.

`-nw, --nowindows`
> Force the use of the command-line interface, even if a windows interface is available.

`-p` *pidnum*, `-c` *pidnum*, `--pid` *pidnum*
> Attach to running process *pidnum*.

`-q, --quiet, --silent`
> Do not print the version number on startup.

`-r, --readnow`
> Fully read symbol files on first access.

`-s` *file*, `--symbols` *file*
> Read symbols from *file*.

`--se` *file*
> Use *file* for both the symbol file and the executable file.

`--statistics`
> Print statistics about CPU time and memory usage after each command finishes.

`-t` *device*, `--tty` *device*
> Use *device* for input/output by the program being debugged.

`--tui`
> Use the Terminal User Interface (TUI).

`-x` *file*, `--command` *file*
> Execute GDB commands from *file*.

`--version`
> Print version information and then exit.

`-w, --windows`
> Force the use of a window interface if there is one.

`--write`
> Allow writing into executable and core files.

Initialization Files

Two files are used to initialize GDB and the *readline* library, respectively.

The .gdbinit File

At startup, GDB reads its *initialization file*. This is a file of commands, such as option settings, for example, that you tell GDB to run every time it starts up. The initialization file is named *.gdbinit* on Unix (BSD, Linux, etc.) systems. Some MS-Windows versions of GDB use *gdb.ini* instead. Empty lines (they do nothing) are allowed, and comments in initialization files start with a # and continue to the end of the line. GDB executes commands from initialization files and from the command line in the following order:

1. Commands in *$HOME/.gdbinit*. This acts as a "global" initialization; settings that should always be used go here.

2. Command-line options and operands.

3. Commands in *./.gdbinit*. This allows for option settings that apply to a particular program by keeping the file in the same directory as the program's source code.

4. Command files specified with the -x option.

You may use the -nx option to make GDB skip the execution of the initialization files.

The .inputrc File

Just like the Bash shell, GDB uses the *readline* library to provide command-line history and editing. You may use either vi- or Emacs-style commands for editing your command line. The *readline* library reads the file *~/.inputrc* to initialize its settings and options. The details are beyond the scope of

---

this book; see the Bash and GDB documentation or the online Info system for the full story. Here is a sample *.inputrc* file:

`set editing-mode vi`	*Use vi editor commands*
`set horizontal-scroll-mode On`	*Scroll line left/right as cursor moves along it*
`control-h: backward-delete-char`	*Use ^H as backspace character*
`set comment-begin #`	*For Bash, # starts comments*
`set expand-tilde On`	*Expand ~ notation*
`"\C-r": redraw-current-line`	*Make ^R redraw the current input line*

GDB Expressions

GDB can be thought of as a specialized programming language. It has variables and operators similar to those of C, and special features for debugging. This section looks at the different kinds of expressions that GDB understands.

The Value History

Every time you print a value with print, GDB saves the value in the *value history*. You can reference these saved values by their numeric place in the history, preceded with a $. GDB reminds you of this by printing $n = val. For example:

```
$ gdb whizprog
...
(gdb) print stopped_early
$1 = 0
(gdb) print whiny_users
$2 = TRUE
(gdb)
```

A plain $ refers to the most recent value in the value history. This can save considerable typing. If you've just looked at a pointer variable, you can use:

```
(gdb) print *$
```

to print the contents of whatever the pointer is pointing to. $$ refers to the next most recent value in the history, and $$n refs to the value *n* places from the end. (Thus, $n counts from the beginning, while $$n counts from the end.)

You can use show values to see the values in the history. Whenever GDB reloads the executable (rereads the symbol table), it clears the value history. This is because the value history may have contained pointers into the symbol table and such pointers become invalid when the symbol table is reloaded.

Convenience Variables and Machine Registers

GDB lets you create *convenience variables*. These are variables you can use to store values as you need them. Their names begin with a $ and consist of alphanumeric characters and underscores. They should start with a letter or underscore. (Note that values in the value history have names that are numeric.) You might want to use a convenience variable as an array index:

```
(gdb) set $j = 0
(gdb) print data[$j++]
```

After these two commands, simply hitting the ENTER key repeats the last command, stepping through the array one element at a time.

GDB predefines several convenience variables. It also enables you to access the machine registers using predefined register names. Register names vary with machine architecture, of course, but there are four predefined registers available on every architecture.

The following list summarizes the convenience variables and predefined registers. The last four entries in the list are the registers that are always available.

$	The most recent value in the value history.
$n	Item *n* in the value history.
$$	The next to last item in the value history.

$$n	Item *n* in the value history, counting from the end.
$_	The address last printed by the x command.
$__	The *contents* of the address last printed by the x command.
$_exitcode	The exit status that the debuggee returned when it exited.
$bpnum	The breakpoint number of the most recently set breakpoint.
$cdir	The compilation directory for the current source file, if one is recorded in the object file.
$cwd	The current working directory.
$fp	The frame pointer register.
$pc	The program counter register.
$ps	The processor status register.
$sp	The stack pointer register.

Special Expressions

GDB understands the syntax (types, operators, operator precedence) of the language being debugged. You can use the same syntax to enter expressions as you do to modify GDB convenience variables (such as $i++). GDB also understands several special syntaxes that let you do things that are not in the target language, as follows:

Array constants

You can create an array constant in the debuggee's memory by enclosing a list of element values in braces. For example, { 1, 2, 3, 42, 57 }.

Array operator

The @ array operator prints all the elements of an array up to a given subscript. For example, if your program uses malloc( ) to allocate memory:

```
double *vals = malloc(count * sizeof(double));
```

you can print a single element using regular subscripting:

```
(gdb) print vals[3]
$1 = 9
```

However, you can access vals[0] through vals[2] with:

```
(gdb) print *vals@3
$2 = {0, 1, 4}
```

File resolution

If you use the same variable name in several source files (for example, each one is static), you can specify which one you mean using *file*::*variable*. For example:

```
(gdb) print 'main.c'::errcount
$2 = 0
```

It is necessary to put main.c in single quotes to avoid ambiguity with the C++ :: operator.

The GDB Text User Interface

GDB, in its default mode, shows its line-oriented heritage. When single-stepping, it displays only one line of source code at a time. Graphical debuggers can show you much more, and indeed many programmers prefer a graphical debugger, if only for this reason. However, recent versions of GDB offer a text user interface (TUI), which uses the tried-and-true *curses* library to provide several "windows" on a regular terminal or terminal emulator, such as an xterm. This can be quite effective, especially since it allows you to do *everything* from the keyboard.

A number of set options and GDB commands are specific to the TUI. These are listed along with the rest of the set options and GDB commands in the later section "Summary of set and show Commands," and in the later section "Alphabetical Summary of GDB Commands."

Unfortunately (as of GDB 6.3), the TUI is still immature; I could not get several documented features to work. Thus this book doesn't provide detailed coverage of it. However, it should improve over time, and you should continue to evaluate it to see whether it meets your needs.

Group Listing of GDB Commands

This section summarizes the GDB commands by task. Esoteric commands, such as those used by GDB's maintainers,

---

or to cross-debug remote systems connected via serial port or a network, have been omitted.

Aliases for Other Commands

Alias	Short for ...	Alias	Short for ...
bt	backtrace	i	info
c	continue	l	list
cont	continue	n	next
d	delete	ni	nexti
dir	directory	p	print
dis	disable	po	print-object
do	down	r	run
e	edit	s	step
f	frame	share	sharedlibrary
fo	forward-search	si	stepi
gcore	generate-core-file	u	until
h	help	where	backtrace

Breakpoints

awatch	Set an expression watchpoint.
break	Set a breakpoint at a line or function.
catch	Set a catchpoint to catch an event.
clear	Clear a given breakpoint.
commands	Specify commands to run when a breakpoint is reached.
condition	Supply a condition to a particular breakpoint.
delete	Delete one or more breakpoints or auto-display expressions.
disable	Disable one or more breakpoints.
enable	Enable one or more breakpoints.
hbreak	Set a hardware-assisted breakpoint.
ignore	Set the ignore-count of a particular breakpoint.

rbreak	Set a breakpoint for all functions matching a regular expression.
rwatch	Set a read watchpoint for an expression.
tbreak	Set a temporary breakpoint.
tcatch	Set a temporary catchpoint.
thbreak	Set a temporary hardware-assisted breakpoint.
watch	Set an expression watchpoint.

Examining Data

call	Call a function in the program.
delete display	Cancel one or more expressions that have been set to display when the program stops.
delete mem	Delete a memory region.
disable display	Disable one or more expressions that have been set to display when the program stops.
disable mem	Disable a memory region.
disassemble	Disassemble a section of memory.
display	Print the value of an expression each time the program stops.
enable display	Enable one or more expressions that have been set to display when the program stops.
enable mem	Enable a memory region.
inspect	Same as print.
mem	Define attributes for a memory region.
output	Similar to print, but doesn't save the value in history and doesn't print a newline. For scripting.
print	Print the value of an expression.
print-object	Cause an Objective C object to print information about itself.
printf	Print values such as the printf command.
ptype	Print the definition of a given type.
set	Evaluate an expression and save the result in a program variable.
set variable	Same as set, avoids conflict with GDB variables.
undisplay	Cancel one or more expressions that have been set to display when the program stops.
whatis	Print the data type of an expression.
x	Examine memory: x/fmt address. See the entry for **x** in the later section "Alphabetical Summary of GDB Commands."

Controlling and Examining Files

add-symbol-file
    Add symbols from a dynamically loaded file to GDB's symbol table.

add-symbol-file-from-memory
    Load the symbols from a dynamically loaded object file in the debuggee's memory.

cd
    Set the current directory for GDB and the debuggee.

core-file
    Specify a file to use as the core dump for memory and register contents.

directory
    Add a directory to the beginning of the source file search path.

edit
    Edit a file or function.

exec-file
    Specify a file to use as the executable.

file
    Specify the filename of the program to be debugged.

forward-search
    Search forward in the current source file for a regular expression, starting at the last line listed.

generate-core-file
    Create a core file from the current state of the debuggee.

list
    List a function or line.

nosharedlibrary
    Unload all shared object library symbols.

path
> Add one or more directories to the object file search path.

pwd
> Print the current directory.

reverse-search
> Search backward in the current source file for a regular expression, starting at the last line listed.

search
> Same as forward-search.

section
> Change the base address of a particular section in the exec file.

sharedlibrary
> Load shared object library symbols for files matching a regular expression.

symbol-file
> Load symbol table information from a specified executable file.

Running a Program

advance	Continue the program up to the given location.
attach	Attach to a process or file outside of GDB.
continue	Continue the program being debugged.
detach	Detach a previously attached process or file.
finish	Execute until selected stack frame returns.
handle	Specify how to handle a signal.
interrupt	Interrupt the execution of the debugged program.
jump	Continue the program being debugged at specified line or address.
kill	Kill the program being debugged.

next	Execute the program's next statement.
nexti	Execute the program's next instruction.
run	Start the debugged program.
signal	Continue the program, giving it a specified signal.
start	Run the debugged program until the beginning of the main procedure. Useful for C++ where constructors run before main( ).
step	Step the program until it reaches a different source line. Descends into called functions.
stepi	Step exactly one instruction.
thread	Switch between threads.
thread apply	Apply a command to a list of threads.
thread apply all	Apply a command to all threads.
tty	Set the terminal for future runs of the debuggee.
unset environment	Remove a variable from the debuggee's environment.
until	Execute until the program reaches a source line greater than the current one.

Examining the Stack

backtrace	Print a backtrace of all stack frames.
down	Select and print the stack frame called by the current one.
frame	Select and print a stack frame.
return	Make selected stack frame return to its caller.
select-frame	Select a stack frame without printing anything.
up	Select and print the stack frame that called the current one.

Status Inquiries

info	General command for showing information about the debuggee.
macro	Prefix for commands dealing with C preprocessor macros.
show	General command for showing information about the debugger.

Support Facilities

apropos	Search for commands matching a regular expression.
complete	List the command completions for the rest of the line.
define	Define a new command.
document	Document a user-defined command.
dont-repeat	Don't repeat this command. For use in user-defined commands.
down-silently	Same as the down command, but doesn't print messages.
echo	Print a constant string.
else	Provide a list of alternative commands for use with if.
end	End a list of commands or actions.
help	Print a list of commands.
if	Execute nested commands once if the conditional expression is nonzero.
make	Run the make program using the rest of the line as arguments.
quit	Exit GDB.
shell	Execute the rest of the line as a shell command.
source	Read commands from a named file.
up-silently	Same as the up command, but doesn't print messages.
while	Execute nested commands while the conditional expression is nonzero.

Text User Interface Commands

focus	Change which window receives the keyboard focus.
layout	Change the layout of the windows in use.
refresh	Clear and redraw the screen.
tui reg	Change which registers are shown in the register window.
update	Update the source window.
winheight	Change the height of a particular window.

Frequently Used Commands

GDB offers a bewilderingly large number of commands, but most users can get by with just a small handful. Table 1 lists the ones that you are likely to use most often.

Table 1. The top dozen GDB commands

Command	Purpose	Examples
backtrace	Show call trace	ba
break	Set breakpoint at routine entry or at line number	b main b parser.c:723
continue	Continue from breakpoint	cont
delete	Remove breakpoint	d 3
finish	Step until end of routine	fin
info breakpoints	List current breakpoints	i br
next	Step to next statement and over routine calls	ne
print	Print expression	print 1.0/3.0
run	(Re)run program, optionally with arguments	ru ru -u -o foo < data
step	Step to next statement and into routines	s
x	Examine memory	x/s *environ
until	Continue execution until reaching a source line	until until 2367

Summary of set and show Commands

The set command accepts a large number of different parameters that control GDB's behavior. Many of the accepted parameters are rather esoteric. The show command

---

displays the values of the same parameters as set accepts. The following section summarizes the parameters and how they affect GDB.

For most of the options, set *option* and set *option* on are equivalent; they enable the option. Use set *option* off to disable the option.

annotate

```
set annotate level
show annotate
```

Set the annotation_level variable to *level*. GUI programs that call GDB as a subsidiary process use this variable.

architecture

```
set architecture architecture
show architecture
```

Set the architecture of target to *architecture*. Primarily used in cross-debugging.

args

```
set args
show args
```

Give the debuggee the argument list when you start it. The run command uses this list when it isn't given any arguments. See the entry for **run** in the later section "Alphabetical Summary of GDB Commands."

auto-solib-add

```
set auto-solib-add
show auto-solib-add
```

Automatically load symbols from shared libraries as needed. When set to off, symbols must be loaded manually with the sharedlibrary command.

auto-solib-limit

```
set auto-solib-limit megs
show auto-solib-limit
```

Limit the size of symbols from shared libraries that will be automatically loaded to *megs* megabytes. Not available on all systems.

---

backtrace

```
set backtrace limit count
show backtrace limit
set backtrace past-main
show backtrace past-main
```

The first syntax limits the number of stack frames shown in a backtrace to *count*. The default is unlimited. The second syntax controls whether GDB shows information about frames that precede the main( ) function. Such *startup* code is usually not of interest, thus the default is off.

breakpoint

```
set breakpoint pending val
show breakpoint pending
```

How GDB should handle breakpoint locations that can't be found (for example, if a shared library has yet to be loaded). Values are on, off, or auto. When *val* is on, GDB automatically creates a pending breakpoint. For auto, it asks you. For off, pending breakpoints are not created.

can-use-hw-watchpoints

```
set can-use-hw-watchpoints value
show can-use-hw-watchpoints
```

If nonzero, GDB uses hardware support for watchpoints, if the system has such support. Otherwise, it doesn't.

case-sensitive

```
set case-sensitive
show case-sensitive
```

Set whether GDB should ignore case when searching for symbols. This variable can be set to on, off, or auto. For auto, the case sensitivity depends upon the language.

coerce-float-to-double

```
set coerce-float-to-double
show coerce-float-to-double
```

When calling a function that is not prototyped, if this variable is on, GDB coerces values of type float to type double. If the variable is off, floats are not coerced to double and prototyped functions receive float values as is.

commands

commands

```
show commands [cmdnum]
show commands +
```

By default, show the last 10 commands in the command history. With a numeric *cmdnum*, show the 10 commands centered around *cmdnum*. The second syntax shows the 10 commands following those just printed.

complaints

```
set complaints limit
show complaints
```

When GDB encounters problems reading in symbol tables, it normally does not complain. By setting this variable, GDB produces up to *limit* complaints about each kind of problem it finds. The default is 0, which creates no complaints. Use a large number to mean "unlimited."

confirm

```
set confirm
show confirm
```

GDB normally asks for confirmation before certain operations, such as deleting breakpoints. Set this value to off to disable confirmation. Do this only if you're really sure that you know what you're doing.

convenience

```
show convenience
```

Print a list of convenience variables used so far, along with their values. Can be abbreviated to show conv.

copying

```
show copying
```

Display the GNU General Public License (GPL).

cp-abi

```
set cp-abi
show cp-abi
```

The Application Binary Interface (ABI) used for inspecting C++ objects. The default is auto, where GDB determines the ABI on its own. Other acceptable values are gnu-v2 for g++ versions before 3.0, gnu-v3 for g++ versions 3.0 and later, and hpaCC for the HP ANSI C++ compiler.

debug-file-directory

```
set debug-file-directory dir
show debug-file-directory
```

Look in *dir* for separate debugging information files. For use on systems where debugging information is not included in executable files.

demangle-style

```
set demangle-style style
show demangle-style
```

Choose the scheme used to convert a "mangled" name back into the original Objective C or C++ name. Available values for *style* are:

arm	Use the algorithm given in *The Annotated C++ Reference Manual*. The GDB documentation warns that this setting alone does not allow debugging of code produced by cfront.[a]
auto	GDB attempts to figure out the demangling style.
gnu	Use the same scheme as that of the GNU C++ compiler (g++). This is the default.
hp	Use the scheme of HP's ANSI C++ compiler, aCC.
lucid	Use the scheme from Lucid's C++ compiler, lcc.

[a] In practice this isn't likely to be an issue; cfront-based C++ compilers are no longer common.

directories

```
show directories
```

Print the current search path of directories that contain source files.

disassembly-flavor

```
set disassembly-flavor flavor
show disassembly-flavor
```

The current instruction set for printing machine-level instructions. This command is currently defined only for the Intel x86 architecture. The *flavor* is either intel or att; the default is att.

editing

```
set editing
show editing
```

Enable editing of command lines as they are typed.

environment

```
set environment variable[=value]
show environment [variable]
```

Set environment variable *variable* to optional *value* or to the empty string. With no *variable*, show the entire environment. Otherwise, show the value of the given *variable*.

exec-done-display

```
set exec-done-display
show exec-done-display
```

Enable notification of completion for asynchronous execution commands.

extension-language

```
set extension-language .ext lang
show extension-language
```

Associate filename extension *.ext* with programming language *lang*.

follow-fork-mode

```
set follow-fork-mode mode
show follow-fork-mode
```

Choose which process GDB should continue to debug when the debuggee creates a new process. The value of *mode* is parent if GDB should follow the parent, or child if GDB should follow the child.

gnutarget

```
set gnutarget format
show gnutarget
```

The current file format of the debuggee (core file, executable, .o file). The default is auto, and is probably best left that way.

height

```
set height count
show height
```

The number of lines GDB thinks are in a page. Use 0 to keep GDB from pausing.

history

```
set history feature
show history feature
```

Control different aspects of GDB's command history. Values and meanings for *feature* are as follows:

```
set history expansion
show history expansion
```

> Use csh-style ! commands for history operations. The default is off.

```
set history filename file
show history filename
```

> Save the command history to *file*, and restore it from there upon startup. This overrides the default filename, which is taken from the value of the environment variable GDBHIST-FILE if it is set. Otherwise, the default filename is *./.gdb_history*.

```
set history save
show history save
```

> Enable saving/restoring of the command history.

```
set history size amount
show history size
```

> Limit the number of saved history commands to *amount*.

input-radix

```
set input-radix base
show input-radix
```

The default input radix for entering numbers. Acceptable values for *base* are 8, 10, and 16. The value must be entered unambiguously (leading 0 for octal, leading 0x or 0X for hexadecimal), or in the current input radix.

language

```
set language lang
show language
```

Set the source language to *lang*. Normally, GDB is able to determine the source language from information in the executable file.

listsize

```
set listsize count
show listsize
```

The number of source lines GDB lists with the list command.

logging

```
set logging
set logging option value
show logging
```

With the usual on and off values, set logging enables and disables logging of GDB command output. With an *option* and *value*, the particular logging option is set to *value*.

Logging Options

file	The file to which GDB logs command output. The default is *gdb.txt*.
overwrite	If set, overwrite the log file each time. Otherwise, GDB appends to it.
redirect	If set, send output to the log file only. The default outputs to both the terminal and the log file.

max-user-call-depth

```
set max-user-call-depth limit
show max-user-call-depth
```

Set the maximum number of recursive calls to a user-defined command to *limit*. When the limit is exceeded, GDB assumes that the command has gone into infinite recursion and aborts with an error.

opaque-type-resolution

```
set opaque-type-resolution
show opaque-type-resolution
```

Resolve opaque struct/class/union types when loading symbols.
That is, if one file uses a type opaquely (struct foo *), find the
definition for that type in the file that defines it.

osabi

```
set osabi os-abi-type
show osabi
```

The Operating System/Application Binary Interface of the
debuggee. The default is auto, which means GDB figures it out
automatically. Use this if you need to override GDB's guess.

output-radix

```
set output-radix base
show output-radix
```

The default output radix for displaying numbers. Acceptable
values for *base* are 8, 10, and 16. The value must be entered
unambiguously (leading 0 for octal, leading 0x or 0X for hexadecimal), or in the current input radix.

overload-resolution

```
set overload-resolution
show overload-resolution
```

When calling an overloaded function from GDB, search for a
function whose signature matches the types of the arguments.

pagination

```
set pagination
show pagination
```

Enable/disable pagination of output. Default is on.

paths

```
show paths
```

Display the current search path for executable programs (the
PATH environment variable). This path is also used to find object
files.

print

```
set print print-opt
show print print-opt
```

GDB lets you control the printing of many different aspects of the debuggee. Many of these options are enabled by typing either set print option-name or set print option-name on. Using off instead of on disables the particular printing option. You can use show print option-name to see whether the option's printing setting is on or off. The values for print-opt, and descriptions of GDB's behavior when a particular print-opt is on, are presented in the following list.

set print address, show print address
  Include the program counter in stack frame information.

set print array, show print array
  Prettyprint arrays. This is easier to read but takes up more space. Default is off.

set print asm-demangle, show print asm-demangle
  Demangle C++/Objective C names, even in disassembly listings.

set print demangle, show print demangle
  Demangle C++/Objective C names in output.

set print elements count, show print elements
  Print no more than count elements from an array. The default is 200; a value of 0 means "unlimited."

set print null-stop, show print null-stop
  Stop printing array elements upon encountering one set to zero (ASCII NUL for character arrays, hence the name). Default is off.

set print object, show print object
  For a pointer, print the pointed-to object's actual type, which is derived from virtual function table information, instead of the declared type. The default is off, which prints the declared type.

set print pascal_static-members
show print pascal_static-members
  Print Pascal static members.

set print pretty, show print pretty
  Prettyprint structures, one element per line, with indentation to convey nesting.

```
set print sevenbit-strings
show print sevenbit-strings
```
Print 8-bit characters in strings as *nnn*.

```
set print static-members
show print static-members
```
Print static members when displaying a C++ object.

```
set print symbol-filename
show print symbol-filename
```
When printing the symbolic form of an address, include the source filename and line number.

```
set print union, show print union
```
Print unions inside structures.

```
set print vtbl, show print vtbl
```
Prettyprint C++ virtual function tables. The default is off.

```
set print max-symbolic-offset max
show print max-symbolic-offset
```
When displaying addresses, only use the *symbol + offset* form if the offset is less than *max*. The default is 0, which means "unlimited."

prompt

```
set prompt string
show prompt
```

Set GDB's prompt to *string*, or show the prompt string. The default prompt is (gdb).

radix

```
set radix base
show radix
```

Set the input and output radixes to the same number. Acceptable values for *base* are 8, 10, and 16. The value must be entered unambiguously (leading 0 for octal, leading 0x or 0X for hexadecimal), or in the current input radix. See also **input-radix** and **output-radix**.

scheduler-locking

```
set scheduler-locking
show scheduler-locking
```

On some operating systems, control the scheduling of other threads (those not being traced) in the debuggee. The value is one

of on, off, or step. If set to off, all threads run, with the chance
that a different thread could pre-empt the debugger (hit a breakpoint, catch a signal, etc.). When set to on, GDB allows only the
current thread to run. When set to step, the scheduler locks only
during single-stepping operations.

solib-absolute-prefix

```
set solib-absolute-prefix path
show solib-absolute-prefix
```

Use *path* as the prefix for any absolute paths to shared libraries.
This is mainly useful for cross-debugging, to find the target's
shared libraries when debugging on a host.

solib-search-path

```
set solib-search-path path
show solib-search-path
```

Search the colon-separated list of directories in *path* to find a
shared library. GDB searches this path after trying solib-
absolute-prefix. This too is mainly useful for cross-debugging.

step-mode

```
set step-mode
show step-mode
```

Set the mode of the step command. By default, step does not
enter functions that lack debugging information. Setting this variable to on causes GDB to enter such functions, allowing you to
examine the machine level instructions.

stop-on-solib-events

```
set stop-on-solib-events
show stop-on-solib-events
```

Stop when a shared library event occurs. The most common such
events are the loading and unloading of a shared library.

symbol-reloading

```
set symbol-reloading
show symbol-reloading
```

On systems that support automatic relinking (such as VxWorks),
reload the symbol table when an object file has changed.

trust-readonly-sections

```
set trust-readonly-sections
show trust-readonly-sections
```

Believe that read-only sections will remain read-only. This allows GDB to fetch the contents from the object file, instead of from a possibly remote debuggee. This is useful primarily for remote debugging.

tui

```
set tui feature value
show tui feature
```

Set the TUI feature *feature* to *value*.

TUI Features

```
set tui active-border-mode mode
show tui active-border-mode
```
> Choose/show the *curses* library attribute for the border of the active window. Available choices are normal, standout, half, half-standout, bold, and bold-standout.

```
set tui border-kind kind
show tui border-kind
```
> Set/show the characters used to draw the border to one of the following:

acs	Draw borders using the Alternate Character Set (line-drawing characters) if the terminal supports it.
ascii	Draw borders using the regular characters +, -, and |.
space	Draw borders using space characters.

```
set tui border-mode mode
show tui border-mode
```
> Choose/show the *curses* library attribute for the border of the other, nonactive windows. Available choices are normal, standout, half, half-standout, bold, and bold-standout.

values

```
show values [valnum]
show values +
```

With no arguments, print the last 10 values in the value history (for more on this, see the earlier section "The Value History").

With *valnum*, print 10 values centered around that value history item number. With +, print 10 more saved values following the one most recently printed.

variable

```
set variable assignment
```

Ensure that *assignment* actually affects a program variable instead of a GDB variable.

verbose

```
set verbose
show verbose
```

Enable display of informative messages during long operations. This reassures you that GDB is still alive.

version

```
show version
```

Show the current version of GDB.

warranty

```
show warranty
```

Display the "no warranty" provisions from the GNU General Public License (GPL).

watchdog

```
set watchdog seconds
show watchdog
```

Wait no more than *seconds* seconds for a remote target to finish a low-level stepping or continuation operation. If the timeout expires, GDB reports an error.

width

```
set width numchars
show width
```

Set the number of characters allowed in a line. Use a value of 0 to keep GDB from wrapping long lines.

write

```
set write
show write
```
Allow GDB to write into the executable and core files. The default is off.

Summary of the info Command

The info command displays information about the state of the debuggee (as opposed to show, which provides information about internal GDB features, variables, and options). With no arguments, it provides a list of possible features about which information is available.

info ...	Information displayed
address *sym*	Information about where symbol *sym* is stored. This is either a memory address or a register name.
all-registers	Information about all registers, including floating-point registers.
args	Information about the arguments to the current function (stack frame).
break [*bpnum*]	Information about breakpoint *bpnum* if given, or about all breakpoints if not.
breakpoints [*bpnum*]	Same information as the info break command.
catch	Information on exception handlers active in the current frame.
classes [*regexp*]	Information about Objective-C classes that match *regexp*, or about all classes if *regexp* is not given.
display	Information about items in the automatic display list.
extensions	Information about the correspondence of filename extensions to source code programming languages.
f [*address*]	Same information as the info frame command.
files	Information about the current debugging target, including the current executable, core, and symbol files.
float	Information about the floating-point hardware.

info ...	Information displayed
frame [*address*]	With no argument, print information about the current frame. With an *address*, print information about the frame containing *address*, but do not make it the current frame.
functions [*regexp*]	With no argument, print the names and types of all functions. Otherwise, print information about functions whose names match *regexp*.
handle	The list of all signals and how GDB currently treats them.
line *line-spec*	The starting and ending address for the code containing the line specified by *line-spec*. See **list** in the "Alphabetical Summary of GDB Commands" section for a description of *line-spec*. This sets the default address to the starting address for the given line, so that x/i may be used to examine instructions.
locals	Information about local variables (static or automatic) accessible from the current frame.
macro *macroname*	Show the definition and source location for the macro *macroname*.
mem	Information about memory regions and their attributes.
proc [*item*]	Information about the running debuggee. Available on systems that supply */proc*. The optional *item* is one of: mappings for available address ranges and how they may be accessed, times for starting time and user and system CPU time, id for process ID information, status for general status of the process, or all for all of the above.
program	Information about the running debuggee, such as running or stopped, and the process ID.
registers [*reg ...*]	With no arguments, information about all machine registers except floating-point registers. Otherwise, information about the named registers.
s	Same information as the info stack command (which is the same as the backtrace command).
scope *address*	Information about variables local to the scope containing *address*, which can be a function name, source line, or absolute address preceded by *.
selectors [*regexp*]	Information about Objective-C selectors that match *regexp*, or about all selectors if *regexp* is not given.
set	Same as the show command with no arguments.

info ...	Information displayed
share	Same as the info sharedlibrary command.
sharedlibrary	Information about currently loaded shared libraries.
signal	Same as the info handle command.
source	Information about the source file, such as compilation directory, programming language, and debugging information.
sources	Information about all source files that have debugging information. The output is split into two lists: those whose information has already been read, and those whose information will be read when needed.
stack	Same information as the backtrace command.
symbol address	The name of the symbol (function, variable, etc.) stored at address address.
target	Identical to the info files command.
terminal	Current terminal modes settings.
threads	All the program's current threads.
types [regexp]	Information about types that match regexp, or about all types in the program if regexp is not given.
variables [regexp]	With no argument, print the names and types of all variables except for local variables. Otherwise, print information about variables whose names match regexp.
watchpoints [wpnum]	Information about watchpoint wpnum, or about all watchpoints if wpnum is not given.
win	The names and sizes of all displayed TUI windows.

Alphabetical Summary of GDB Commands

The following alphabetical summary of GDB commands includes all those that are useful for day-to-day debugging. Esoteric commands, such as those used by GDB's maintainers, or to cross-debug remote systems connected via serial port or a network, have been omitted.

Many of these commands may be abbreviated. The list of abbreviations is provided in the earlier section "Aliases for Other Commands."

add-symbol-file

```
add-symbol-file file addr [-mapped] [-readnow]
add-symbol-file file [-s section address ...]
```

Read additional symbol table information from *file*, which was dynamically loaded into the debuggee outside of GDB's knowledge. You must tell GDB the address at which it was loaded, since GDB cannot determine this on its own. The -mapped and -readnow options are the same as for the file command; see **file** for more information. You may use -s to name the memory starting at *address* with the name *section*. You can provide multiple *section/address* pairs with multiple -s options.

advance

```
advance bp-spec
```

Continue executing until the program reaches *bp-spec*, which can have any value acceptable to the break command (see **break** for the details). This command is like the until command, but it does not skip recursive function calls, and the location doesn't have to be in the current frame.

apropos

```
apropos regex
```

Search through the built-in documentation for commands that match the regular expression *regex*. Multiple words constitute a single regular expression. GDB uses Basic Regular Expressions (like those of grep); however, it also ignores case when matching.

attach

```
attach pid
```

Attach to the running process *pid*, and use it to obtain information about in-memory data. You must have appropriate permission to attach to a running process.

awatch

`awatch` *expression*

Set a watchpoint to stop when *expression* is either read or written. (Compare **rwatch** and **watch**.)

backtrace

`backtrace [`*count*`]`

Print a full list of all stack frames. With a positive *count*, print only the innermost *count* stack frames. With a negative *count*, print only the outermost *count* stack frames.

break

```
break [bp-spec]
break bp-spec if condition
break bp-spec thread threadnum
break bp-spec thread threadnum if condition
```

Set a breakpoint. The first form sets an unconditional breakpoint; execution of the debuggee stops when the breakpoint is reached. The second form sets a conditional breakpoint: when the breakpoint is reached, GDB evaluates the *condition*. If the condition is true, execution stops. If it isn't, the program continues. In either case, *bp-spec* is one of the items given in the following section.

The third and fourth forms are similar to the first and second ones respectively; however, they work on individual threads of control running within the debuggee. They specify that GDB should stop the program only when the given thread *threadnum* reaches the point specified by *bp-spec*.

Breakpoint Specifications

The following list shows the different forms that the break command can take.

break

> Set a breakpoint at the next instruction in the current stack frame. If you are not in the innermost stack frame, control stops as soon as execution returns to that frame. This is like the `finish` command, except that `finish` doesn't leave a breakpoint set. In the innermost frame, GDB stops when the breakpoint is reached. This is most useful inside loop bodies.

break *function*
> Set a breakpoint at the first instruction of *function*.

break *linenumber*
> Set a breakpoint at line *linenumber* in the current file.

break *file:line*
> Set a breakpoint at line number *line* in source file *file*.

break *file:function*
> Set a breakpoint at function *function* in source file *file*.

break *+offset*
break *-offset*
> Set a breakpoint at *offset* lines forward (*+offset*) or backward (*-offset*) from where execution stopped in the current stack frame.

break **address*
> Set a breakpoint at *address*. This is useful for parts of the object file that don't have debugging symbols available (such as inside shared libraries).

A breakpoint set at a line or statement stops when the first instruction in that statement is reached.

call

call *expression*

Call a function within the debuggee. *expression* is a function name and parameter list. Non-void results are printed and saved in the value history.

catch

catch *event*

Place a catchpoint. Execution stops when the specified *event* occurs.

Catchpoint Events

catch
> A C++ exception is caught.

exec
> The program calls execve( ). This is not implemented on all systems.

fork
>   The program calls fork(). This is not implemented on all systems.

throw
>   A C++ exception is thrown.

vfork
>   The program calls vfork(). This is not implemented on all systems.

cd

cd *dir*

Change GDB's working directory to *dir*.

clear

clear [*bp-spec*]

Clear a breakpoint. The argument is the same as for the break command (see **break**).

commands

commands [*bp*]
... *commands* ...
end

Supply GDB commands that should run when the program stops at a given breakpoint. With no *bp*, the list of commands is associated with the most recent breakpoint, watchpoint, or catchpoint that was *set*, not the one that was most recently *executed*. To clear a list of commands, supply the commands keyword and follow it immediately with end.

complete

complete *prefix*

Show possible command completions for *prefix*. This is intended for Emacs when running GDB in an Emacs buffer.

condition

condition *bp*
condition *bp* *expression*

Add or remove a condition to a given breakpoint. The first syntax removes any condition associated with breakpoint number *bp*. The second form adds *expression* as a condition for breakpoint number *bp*, similar to the break ... if command. See also **break**.

continue

```
continue [count]
```

Resume execution after stopping at a breakpoint. If supplied, *count* is an *ignore count*; see the entry for **ignore**.

core-file

```
core-file [filename]
```

With no argument, indicate that there is no separate *core* file. Otherwise, treat *filename* as the file to use as a *core* file; that is, a file containing a dump of memory from an executing program.

define

```
define commandname
... commands ...
end
```

Create a user-defined command named *commandname*. The series of *commands* makes up the definition of *commandname*. Whenever you type *commandname*, GDB executes the *commands*. This is similar to functions or procedures in regular programming languages. See also **document**.

Hooks

If *commandname* has the form hook-*command*, where *command* is a built-in GDB command, when you enter *command*, GDB runs *commandname* before it runs *command*.

Similarly, if *commandname* has the form hookpost-*command*, then GDB runs the provided sequence of commands after *command* finishes. You thus have available both pre- and post-execution hook facilities.

Finally, for the purposes of providing hooks, GDB recognizes a pseudocommand named stop that "executes" every time the debuggee stops. This allows you to define a hook of the form hook-stop in order to execute a sequence of commands every time the program stops.

delete

```
delete [breakpoints] [range ...]
delete display dnums ...
delete mem mnums ...
```

For the first syntax, remove the given *range* of breakpoints, watchpoints, or catchpoints. With no arguments, delete all breakpoints.

(GDB may prompt for confirmation depending upon the setting of set confirm.) The second syntax removes items from the automatic display list (created with display); see **display** for more information. The third syntax removes defined memory regions created with mem; see **mem** for more information.

detach

```
detach
```

Detach the debugger from the running process previously attached to with attach.

directory

```
directory [dirname ...]
```

Add *dirname* to the list of directories that GDB searches when attempting to find source files. The directory is added to the *front* of the search path. With no argument, clear the directory search path.

disable

```
disable [breakpoints] [range ...]
disable display dnums ...
disable mem mnums ...
```

With the first syntax, disable the breakpoints in *range*, or all breakpoints if these are not supplied. GDB remembers disabled breakpoints, but they do not affect execution of the debuggee. The second syntax disables item(s) *dnums* in the automatic display list; see **display** for more information. The third syntax disables item(s) *mnums* in the list of defined memory regions; see **mem** for more information.

disassemble

```
disassemble
disassemble pc-val
disassemble start end
```

Print a range of memory addresses as assembly code instructions. With no argument, print the entire current function. One argument is assumed to be a program counter value; the function containing this value is dumped. Two arguments specify a range of addresses to dump, from (and including) *start* up to (but not including) *end*.

display

```
display
display/format expression
```

Add *expression* (usually a variable or address) to the list of values that GDB automatically displays every time the debuggee stops. The *format* is one of the format letters accepted by the x command; see **x** for the full list. The trailing "/" and *format* immediately follow the display command. With no arguments, print the current values of the expressions on the display list.

document

```
document commandname
... text ...
end
```

Provide documentation for the user-defined command *commandname*. The documentation consists of the lines provided in *text*. After executing this command, help *commandname* displays *text*. See also **define**.

dont-repeat

```
dont-repeat
```

This command is designed for use inside user-defined commands (see **define**). It indicates that the user-defined command should not be repeated if the user presses ENTER.

down

```
down count
```

Move down *count* stack frames. Positive values for *count* move towards more recent stack frames. See also **frame** and **up**.

down-silently

```
down-silently count
```

Same as the down command, but doesn't print any messages. This is intended mainly for use in GDB scripts.

echo

```
echo strings ...
```

Print *strings*. You may use the standard C escape sequences to generate nonprinting characters. In particular, you should use \n for newline. Note that unlike the shell-level echo command, GDB's echo does *not* automatically supply a newline. You must explicitly request one if you want it.

edit

```
edit [line-spec]
```

Edit the lines in the source file as specified by *line-spec*. See **list** for values for *line-spec*. With no argument, edit the file containing the most recently listed line. This uses the value of $EDITOR as the editor, or ex if that environment variable is not set.

else

```
else
```

Provide an alternate list of commands to execute if the expression in an if is false. Terminate the commands with end. See **if**.

enable

```
enable [breakpoints] [range ...]
enable [breakpoints] delete range ...
enable [breakpoints] once range ...
enable display dnums ...
enable mem mnums ...
```

The first syntax enables breakpoints; either all breakpoints if no *range* is supplied, or just the given breakpoints. The second syntax enables the specified breakpoints so that they stop the program when they're encountered, but are then deleted. The third syntax enables the specified breakpoints so that they stop the program when encountered, but then become disabled. The fourth syntax enables items in the automatic display list that were previously disabled with disable; for more information, see **display**. The fifth syntax enables items in the list of defined memory regions; for more information, see **mem**.

end

end

Terminate a list of commands provided with keywords commands, define, document, else, if, or while.

exec-file

exec-file [*filename*]

With no argument, discard all information about the executable file. Otherwise, treat *filename* as the file to execute. This command searches $PATH to find the file if necessary.

fg

fg [*count*]

An alias for continue; see **continue**.

file

file
file *filename* [-mapped] [-readnow]

The first syntax causes GDB to discard all its information on both the symbol file and the executable file. The second syntax treats *filename* as the file to be debugged; it is used both for symbol table information and as the program to run for the run command.

The -mapped option causes GDB to write symbol table information into a file named program.syms, from which it can be retrieved for subsequent debugging runs. As long as the program hasn't changed, this is faster than reading the symbol table from the executable.

The -readnow option forces GDB to load symbol table information immediately instead of waiting until information is needed.

finish

finish

Continue execution until the current stack frame (function) is about to return. This is most useful when you accidentally step into a function (using step) that does not have debugging information in it (such as a library function).

focus

```
focus window
```

Change the focus to TUI window *window*. Acceptable values for *window* are next, prev, src, asm, regs, and cmd.

forward-search

```
forward-search regex
```

Search forward from the current line for a line that matches the regular expression *regex*, and print it.

frame

```
frame
frame frame-num
frame address
```

Select or print information about the current stack frame (function invocation). Frame zero is the innermost (most recent) stack frame. With no arguments, print the current stack frame. With a *frame-num*, move to that frame. This is the most common kind of argument. An *address* argument may be used to select the frame at the given address. This is necessary if the chaining of stack frames has been damaged by a bug. Some architectures may require more than one *address*.

generate-core-file

```
generate-core-file [file]
```

Generate a core file from the state of the debuggee. With *file*, send the core dump to *file*. Otherwise, use a file named core.*PID*.

handle

```
handle signal keywords ...
```

Set GDB up to handle one or more signals. The *signal* may be a signal number, a signal name (with or without the SIG prefix), a range of the form *low–high*, or the keyword all. The *keywords* are one or more of the following:

ignore	Ignore the signal; do not let the program see it.
noignore	Same as the pass command.
nopass	Same as the ignore command.
noprint	Do not print a message when the signal arrives.
nostop	Do not stop the program when the signal arrives; let the debuggee receive it immediately.

pass	Pass the signal on through to the program.
print	Print a message when the signal arrives.
stop	Stop the program when the signal arrives. Normally, only "error" signals such as SIGSEGV stop the program.

hbreak

hbreak *bp-spec*

Set a hardware-assisted breakpoint. The argument is the same as for the break command (see **break**, earlier in this list). This command is intended for EEPROM/ROM code debugging; it allows you to set a breakpoint at a location without changing the location. However, not all systems have the necessary hardware for this.

help

help [*command*]

With no arguments, print a list of subtopics for which help is available. With *command*, provide help on the given GDB command or group of commands.

if

```
if expression
... commands1 ...
[ else
  ... commands2 ... ]
end
```

Conditionally execute a series of commands. If *expression* is true, execute *commands1*. If an else is present and the expression is false, execute *commands2*.

ignore

ignore *bp count*

Set the ignore count on breakpoint, watchpoint, or catchpoint *bp* to *count*. GDB does not check conditions as long as the ignore count is positive.

inspect

inspect *print-expressions*

An obsolete alias for the print command. See **print** for more information.

info

```
info [feature]
```

Display information about *feature*, which concerns the state of the debuggee. With no arguments, provide a list of features about which information is available. Full details are provided in the section "Summary of the info Command," earlier in this book.

jump

```
jump location
```

Continue execution at *location*, which is either a *line-spec* as for the list command (see **list**), or a hexadecimal address preceded by a *.

The continue command resumes execution where it stopped, while jump moves to a different place. If the *location* is not within the current frame, GDB asks for confirmation since GDB will not change the current setup of the machine registers (stack pointer, frame pointer, etc.).

kill

```
kill
```

Kill the process running the debuggee. This is most useful to force the production of a core dump for later debugging.

layout

```
layout layout
```

Change the layout of the TUI windows to *layout*. Acceptable values for *layout* are:

asm	The assembly window only.
next	The next layout.
prev	The previous layout.
regs	The register window only.
split	The source and assembly windows.
src	The source window only.

The command window is always displayed.

list

```
list function
list line-spec
```

List lines of source code, starting at the beginning of function *function* (first form), or centered around the line defined by *line-spec* (second form). Pressing the ENTER key repeats the last command; for `list`, this shows successive lines of source text. A *line-spec* can take one of the forms shown below.

Line Specifications

list *number*

> List lines centered around line *number*.

list +*offset*
list -*offset*

> List lines centered around the line *offset* lines after (first form) or before (second form) the last line printed.

list *file:line*

> List lines centered around line *line* in source file *file*.

list *file:function*

> List lines centered around the opening brace of function *function* in source file *file*. This is necessary if there are multiple functions of the same name in different source files.

list **address*

> List lines centered around the line containing *address*, which can be an expression.

list *first,last*

> List the lines from *first* to *last*, each of which may be any of the previous forms for a *line-spec*.

list *first,*

> List lines starting with *first*.

list *,last*

> List lines ending with *last*.

list +
list -

> List the lines just after (first form) or just before (second form) the lines just printed.

macro

```
macro expand expression
macro expand-once expression
macro define macro body
macro define macro(args) body
macro undefine macro
```

Work with C preprocessor macros. As of GDB 6.3, not all of these are implemented.

macro expand *expression*

> Display the result of macro expanding *expression*. The results are *not* evaluated, thus they don't need to be syntactically valid. expand may be abbreviated exp.

macro expand-once *expression*

> Expand only those macros whose names appear in *expression* instead of fully expanding all macros. expand-once may be abbreviated exp1. *Not implemented as of GDB 6.3.*

macro define *macro body*
macro define *macro(args) body*

> Define a macro named *macro* with replacement text *body*. As in C and C++, the first form defines a symbolic constant, while the second form defines a macro that accepts arguments. *Not implemented as of GDB 6.3.*

macro undefine *macro*

> Remove the definition of the macro named *macro*. This works only for macros defined with macro define; you cannot undefine a macro in the debuggee. *Not implemented as of GDB 6.3.*

make

```
make [args]
```

Run the make program, passing it *args*. Equivalent to the shell make *args* command. This is useful for rebuilding your program while remaining within GDB.

mem

```
mem start-addr end-addr attributes ...
```

Define a *memory region*—i.e., a portion of the address space starting at *start-addr* and ending at *end-addr* that has particular *attributes*.

Memory Access Attributes

ro	Memory is read-only.
rw	Memory is read-write.
wo	Memory is write-only.
8, 16, 32, 64	GDB should use memory accesses of the specified width in bits. This is often needed for memory-mapped device registers.

next

next [count]

Run the next statement. Unlike step, a function call is treated as a simple statement; single-stepping does not continue inside the called function. With a count, run the next count statements. In any case, execution stops upon reaching a breakpoint or receipt of a signal. See also **step**.

nexti

nexti [count]

Run the next machine instruction. Otherwise, this is similar to the next command in that single-stepping continues *past* a called function instead of into it.

nosharedlibrary

nosharedlibrary

Unload all shared libraries from the debuggee.

output

output expression
output/format expression

Print expression, completely unadorned. No newlines are added, nor is the value preceded by the usual $n =. Neither is the value added to the value history. With "/" and format, output the expression using format, which is the same as for the print command; see **print**.

path

path dir

Add directory dir to the front of the PATH environment variable.

print

```
print [/format] [expression]
```

Print the value of *expression*. If the first argument is "/" and *format*, use the *format* to print the expression. Omitting *expression* prints the previous expression, allowing you to use a different format to see the same value. The allowed *format* values are a subset of the *format* items for the x command; see also **x**, later in this section.

Print Formats

a	Print the value as an address. The address is printed as both an absolute (hexadecimal) address and as an offset from the nearest symbol.
c	Print the value as a character constant.
d	Print the value as a signed decimal integer.
f	Print the value as a floating-point number.
o	Print the value as an octal integer.
t	Print the value as a binary integer (t stands for "two").
u	Print the value as an unsigned decimal integer.
x	Print the value as a hexadecimal integer.

print-object

```
print-object object
```

Cause the Objective-C object *object* to print information about itself. This command may only work with Objective-C libraries that define the hook function _NSPrintForDebugger( ).

printf

```
printf format-string, expressions ...
```

Print *expressions* under control of the *format-string*, as for the C library *printf*(3) function. GDB allows only the simple, single-letter escape sequences (such as \t and \n) to appear in *format-string*.

ptype

```
ptype
ptype expression
ptype type-name
```

Print the full definition of a type. This differs from whatis, in that whatis prints only type names, while ptype gives a full description.

With no argument (the first syntax), print the type of the last value in the value history. This is equivalent to ptype $. With *expression* (the second syntax), print the type of *expression*. Note that the *expression* is not evaluated. No operators with side effects (such as ++, or a function call) execute. The third syntax prints the type of *type-name*, which is either the name of a type or one of the keywords class, enum, struct, or union, followed by a tag. See also **whatis**.

pwd

pwd

Print GDB's current working directory.

quit

quit

Exit GDB.

rbreak

rbreak *regexp*

Set breakpoints on all functions matching the regular expression *regexp*. The regular expression syntax used is that of grep (i.e., Basic Regular Expressions). This is useful for overloaded functions in C++.

refresh

refresh

Redraw and refresh the screen for the TUI. See the earlier section "The GDB Text User Interface" for more information.

return

return [*expression*]

Cause the current stack frame to return to its caller. If provided, *expression* is used at the return value. GDB pops the current stack frame and any below it (functions it called) from the execution stack, causing the returning frame's caller to become the current frame. Execution does *not* resume; the program remains stopped until you issue a continue command.

reverse-search

reverse-search *regex*

Search backwards from the current line for a line that matches the regular expression *regex*, and print it.

run

run [*arguments*]

Run the debuggee, optionally passing it *arguments* as the command-line arguments. GDB also supports simple I/O redirections (<, >, >>); pipes are not supported. GDB remembers the last-used *arguments*; thus a plain run command restarts the program with these same arguments. (Use set args to clear or change the argument list.)

The debuggee receives the arguments you give to the run command, the environment as inherited by GDB and modified by set environment, the current working directory, and the current standard input, standard output, and standard error (unless redirected).

rwatch

rwatch *expression*

Set a watchpoint to stop when *expression* is read. (Compare **awatch** and **watch**.)

search

search *regex*

An alias for forward-search. See **forward-search** for more information.

section

section *sectname address*

Change the base address of *sectname* to *address*. This is a last-ditch command, used when the executable file format doesn't contain data on section addresses or if the data in the file is wrong.

select-frame

```
select-frame
select-frame frame-num
select-frame address
```

Same as the frame command, except that it does not print any messages. See **frame** for more information.

set

```
set [variable]
```

Change the setting either of GDB variables or variables in the debuggee. See the earlier section "Summary of set and show Commands" for more information.

sharedlibrary

```
sharedlibrary [regexp]
```

With no argument, load all the shared libraries required by the program or core file. Otherwise, load only those files whose names match *regexp*.

shell

```
shell [command args]
```

Run the shell command *command* with arguments *args* without leaving GDB. With no arguments, start an interactive subshell.

show

```
show [variable]
```

Show the setting of internal GDB variables. See the earlier section "Summary of set and show Commands" for more information.

signal

```
signal sig
```

Continue the program running, and immediately send it signal *sig*. *sig* may be either a signal number or a signal name. The signal number 0 is special: if the program stops due to receipt of a signal, sending signal 0 resumes it without delivering the original signal.

silent

```
silent
```

Don't print breakpoint-reached messages. Use this command inside a commands list; see **commands**.

source

```
source file
```

Read and execute the commands in *file*. The commands are not printed as they are read, and an error in any one command terminates execution of the file. When executing a command file, commands that normally ask for confirmation do not do so, and many commands that would otherwise print messages are silent.

step

```
step [count]
```

Run the next statement. This differs from the next command in that if the next statement is a function call, step steps into it and continues single-stepping in the called function. However, next calls the function without stepping into it. With a *count*, step through *count* statements. In any case, execution stops upon reaching a breakpoint or receipt of a signal. See also **next**.

stepi

```
stepi [count]
```

Run the next machine instruction. Otherwise, this is similar to the step command in that single-stepping continues into a called function. With a *count*, step through *count* instructions.

symbol-file

```
symbol-file
symbol-file filename [-mapped] [-readnow]
```

With no argument, discard all symbol table information. Otherwise, treat *filename* as the file to get symbol table information from, and as the file to execute. This command searches $PATH to find the file if necessary. The -mapped and -readnow options have the same meaning as for the file command; see **file** for more information.

tbreak

```
tbreak bp-spec
```

Set a temporary breakpoint. The argument is the same as for the break command (see **break**, earlier in this list). The difference is that once the breakpoint is reached, it is removed.

tcatch

```
tcatch event
```

Set a temporary catchpoint. The argument is the same as for the catch command (see **catch**, earlier in this list). The difference is that once the catchpoint is reached, it is removed.

thbreak

```
thbreak bp-spec
```

Set a temporary hardware-assisted breakpoint. The argument is the same as for the hbreak command (see **hbreak**, earlier in this list).

thread

```
thread threadnum
thread apply [threadnum | all] command
```

The first form makes *threadnum* the current thread—i.e., the one with which GDB works. The second form lets you apply *command* to either the specific thread *threadnum* or to all threads.

tty

```
tty device
```

Set the debuggee's input and output to *device* (typically the device file for a terminal).

tui

```
tui reg regkind
```

For the TUI, update the register window to display the register set *regkind*.

Register Sets

The following are the acceptable values for *regkind*.

float	The floating-point registers.
general	The general purpose registers.
next	The "next" register group. Predefined register groups are all, float, general, restore, save, system and vector.
system	The system registers.

undisplay

```
undisplay dnums ...
```

Remove display items *dnums* from the automatic display list. See **display** for more information.

unset

```
unset environment variable
```

Remove environment variable *variable* from the environment passed to the debuggee.

until

```
until [location]
```

Continue execution until it reaches the next source line after the current line. This is most useful for reaching the line after the end of a loop body. Without a *location*, until uses single-stepping to reach the next source line. With a *location*, it uses an internal breakpoint to reach the next source line; this is much faster. The *location* may be any form acceptable to the break command; see **break** for more information.

up

```
up count
```

Move up *count* stack frames. Positive values for *count* move towards less recent stack frames. See also **frame** and **down**.

up-silently

```
up-silently count
```

Same as the up command, but doesn't print any messages. Intended mainly for use in GDB scripts.

update

```
update
```

For the TUI, update the source window and the current execution point.

watch

```
watch expression
```

Set a watchpoint to stop when *expression* is written. (Compare **awatch** and **rwatch**.)

whatis

whatis [*expression*]

With no argument, print the type of the last value in the value history. This is equivalent to whatis $. With *expression*, print the type of *expression*. Note that the *expression* is not evaluated. No operators with side effects (such as ++ or a function call) execute. See also **ptype**.

where

where [*count*]

Identical to the backtrace command; see **backtrace** for more information.

while

while *expression*
... *commands* ...
end

Repeatedly execute a series of commands. As long as *expression* is true, execute *commands*.

winheight

winheight *win* ±*amount*

For the TUI, change the height of window *win* by *amount*. Using + increases the height; using - decreases it. The window name win may be one of asm, cmd, regs, or src.

x

x [[/*NFU*] *addr*]

Examine the data at *address*. Subsequent x commands without an address move forward in memory according to the values for N, F, and U.

The N value is a repeat count, for example, to examine a given number of instructions. The F value is a format, indicating how to print the data. The U value is the unit size in bytes of the items to be displayed.

GBD stores the address printed by the x command in the $_ convenience variable. It stores the *contents* of the address in the $__ convenience variable.

Format Values

    a Print the value as an address. The address is printed as both an absolute (hexadecimal) address and as an offset from the nearest symbol.

    c Print the value as a character constant.

    d Print the value as a signed decimal integer.

    f Print the value as a floating-point number.

    i Print the value as a machine instruction.

    o Print the value as an octal integer.

    s Print the value as a NUL-terminated string.

    t Print the value as a binary integer (t stands for "two").

    u Print the value as an unsigned decimal integer.

    x Print the value as a hexadecimal integer.

Unit Size Values

    b Bytes.

    g Giant words, i.e., 8 bytes.

    h Halfwords, i.e., 2 bytes.

    w Words, i.e., 4 bytes.

Index

We'd like to hear your suggestions for improving our indexes. Send email to
index@oreilly.com.